HAMSTERS

Published by Ringpress Books Limited,
PO Box 8, Lydney, Gloucestershire,
GL15 4YN, United Kingdom.

Design: Sara Howell

First Published 2001

ISBN 1 86054 221 2

Printed in Hong Kong through Printworks Int. Ltd

0 9 8 7 6 5 4 3 2 1

101 FACTS ABOUT HAMSTERS

Julia Barnes

Ringpress Books

1 Ranked as the most popular of all the small animals, the hamster is easy to keep, and makes an ideal children's pet.

2 The word 'hamster' comes from the German word 'hamstern', meaning 'to **hoard**'. This is because hamsters carry food in their cheek pouches and then store it in a burrow.

3 Hamsters belong to the **rodent** family which includes mice, rats, and guinea pigs among its many members.

4 There are 27 assorted types of hamster living in different countries. Most live in hot, dry, desert-like areas.

5 The Syrian or Golden hamster (pictured left), which comes from the deserts of Syria, is the type that most people keep as a pet.

6 Hamsters are **nocturnal**. This means they sleep during the day and become active at night.

7 Even though hamsters are very small, in the wild they travel quite a distance in search of food. They have been known to cover more than 12 miles (20 kms) in one night.

8 Wild hamsters eat seed, some green plants, and occasionally grubs and insects. Supplies can be taken home in the cheek pouches. A Syrian hamster can carry up to half his own body weight in food.

9 Hamsters live in **burrows**. Each burrow has lots of different 'rooms' or compartments, and can be 3 ft (1 m) underground.

10 A 100 years ago, it was thought that the Syrian hamster had died out in the wild. All the many thousands of pet hamsters that we keep today come from a single family of hamsters that were discovered in Syria in 1932.

11 The Syrian hamster measures around 6 ins (15 cms) in length. The females are larger than the males.

12 There is little difference between keeping a male or a female, though some say that males are more easygoing than females.

13 You can expect a Syrian hamster to live for around two years, but some live longer, reaching up to four years of age.

14 The Syrian does not like living with other hamsters. Fights will break out if you try to keep more than one.

15 A different type of hamster, the dwarf hamster, is much more friendly and is happy to live in a small group. The best plan is to keep either two males or two females together.

16 Dwarf Chinese hamsters (pictured left) are still found in the wild in eastern Europe and Asia. They are slightly smaller than the Syrian variety, measuring about 4 ins (11 cms). They live for 18 months to two years.

17 There are two types of Russian Dwarf hamsters. The Dwarf Campbells Russian (pictured above) lives among the sand dunes in Central Asia, Northern Russia and China. He measures 3-4 ins (8-10 cms) and lives for around two years.

18 The Dwarf Winter White Russian (pictured below) comes from eastern Kazakhstan, and north-west Siberia. He measures about 3 ins (8 cms), and lives for 18 months to 2 years.

19 Quick-moving and small, dwarf hamsters are better suited to older children who can handle them more easily.

20 The Roborovski hamster (pictured right) is one for the experts. He is just 2 ins (4-5 cms) in length, and is extremely lively. This is an animal to watch rather than one to handle.

21 The Syrian hamster is famous for his golden colour. But today, you can choose from 100 colours.

22 Single-coloured hamsters (known as **'selfs'**) come in a wide range of goldens, from the palest cream to the deepest honey. They also come in silver-blue, chocolate, lilac, black and tortoiseshell – to name just a few colours.

23 Eye colour can depend on the colour of the coat. For example, you can have a red-eyed cream or a black-eyed cream.

24 There are lots of different coat patterns. The 'marked' varieties may be:

- **Banded**: a white belly with a white band across the back.
- **Roan**: white with coloured hairs.
- **Dominant spot**: white with spots of colour and a white belly.
- **Piebald**: white with coloured spots and patches all over.

25 The Syrian hamster is usually short-haired. But you can also get different types of coat which include:

- **Long-haired** (pictured above): sometimes known as 'Teddy' or 'Angora'.
- **Rex**: the hairs are lifted and slightly curled.
- **Satin**: the coat is smooth and glossy.

26 Hairless hamsters have been developed. They are available in the US where they are known as **Alien** hamsters.

27 Dwarf hamsters are not as colourful as Syrians. The Chinese hamster (pictured below) is usually chestnut brown, with grey ears and a black stripe down his back.

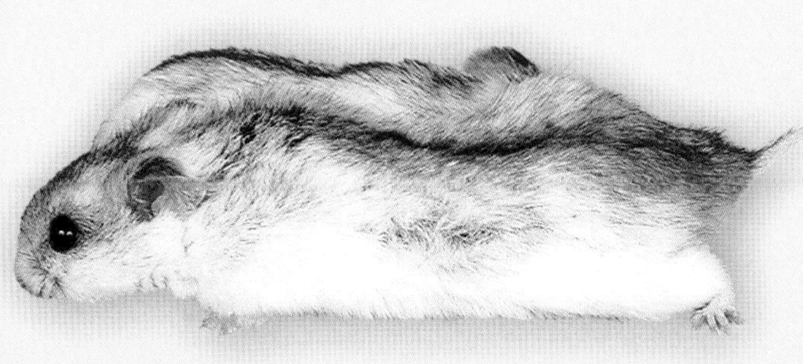

28 The Campbells Russian hamster has a brown-grey coat with a dark brown stripe down his back. The other colours are:

- **Albino**: pure white with red eyes.
- **Opal**: a blue-grey colour.
- **Argente**: a rich orange with a brown-grey stripe along the back.

29 The coat patterns are different from the Syrian. They can be **mottled** (white with patches or spots of colour), and **platinum** (a silver colour).

30 Apart from the normal short-haired coat, the Campbells Russian may have a satin coat or a wavy coat.

31 The Winter White Russian hamster is usually dark grey with a black stripe down his back.

32 In winter, the Winter White turns white (as his name suggests), and so he blends in with the snowy landscape.

33 Breeders have developed a sapphire colour (purple-grey) for the Winter White (pictured left). The stripe down his back is grey.

34 Roborovski hamsters are sandy-coloured with a white belly. This is the only colour they come in at the moment.

35 Hamsters can be bought at pet stores, and experienced staff should be on hand to help you make your choice.

36 If you plan to show your hamster, you will need to go to a hamster breeder who produces the different colours and coats.

37 Most hamsters sleep during the day and become active in the late afternoon and evening. Go to the pet store in the afternoon when you are more likely to see the hamsters in action.

38 You will probably have decided whether you want a male or a female. Ask a member of staff to help you pick out the right one.

39 *Don't* choose a sickly-looking hamster because you feel sorry for him – you could end up with a lot of trouble and heartache trying to get him well.

40 Buy a hamster aged between 5 and 10 weeks, when he can be trained to accept handling.

41 A healthy hamster should show the following signs of good health.

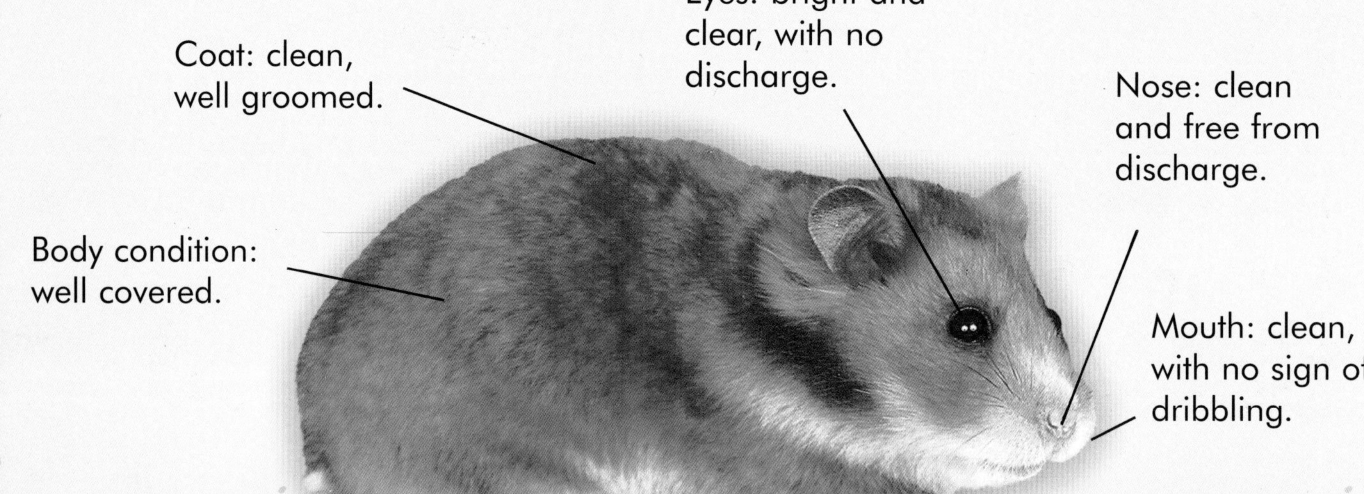

42 Before you bring your hamster home, you must decide where he is going to live. Hamsters need to be kept at a room temperature of 68-72 degrees Fahrenheit (20-22 degrees Centigrade).

43 If the temperature drops below 50 F (10 C), a hamster will go into **hibernation**. This means he will curl up and sleep, and will not wake up again until the temperature rises.

44 Hamsters can catch colds, so make sure your hamster home is raised above ground-level and is not exposed to draughts of cold air.

45 It is nice to have your hamster home on display, but make sure there is enough peace and quiet so your hamster can rest undisturbed.

46 Hamster homes come in all shapes and sizes. The best to buy for a Syrian hamster is a multi-storey plastic unit (pictured above), which gives your hamster an interesting place to live with lots of places to explore.

47 Dwarf hamsters often find the tubes in multi-storey units too wide for them to crawl through, so it is better to choose a glass or plastic tank (pictured below).

48 The tank must have a secure, tight-fitting, wire-mesh lid to prevent attempts to escape.

49 Your hamster will need a nesting box, with nesting material. This can be cotton or shredded tissue paper, such as Kleenexes. Do not use straw, as the sharp spikes can hurt your hamster.

50 The ground area should be covered with softwood shavings (pictured above). First check that these have not been treated with chemicals. Do not use sawdust, as this can irritate the hamster's eyes and nose.

51 Hamsters do not drink a lot, but they must have a supply of fresh water.

52 The best way to provide this is by attaching a gravity-fed water-bottle to your hamster home. Make sure you change the water on a regular basis.

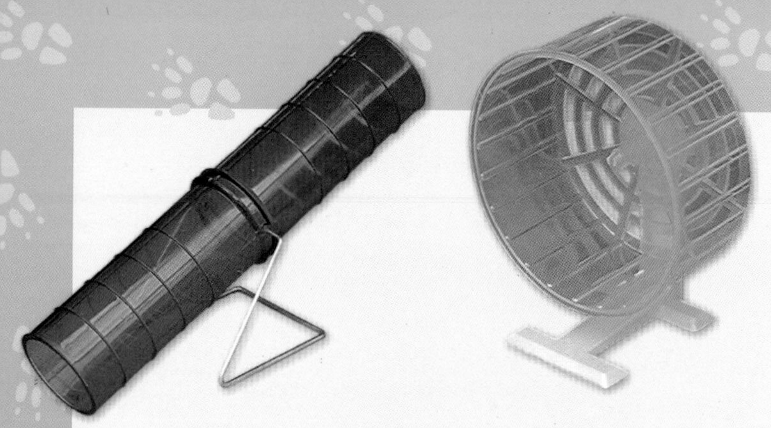

53 There are lots of hamster toys you can buy – tunnels and pipes for exploring, wooden blocks for gnawing, and wheels for exercise sessions.

54 Sometimes the cheapest toys are the best. Your hamster will have great fun going in and out of the cardboard tube from inside a toilet roll – and when that game is over, he can enjoy chewing it up!

55 Hamster balls (pictured below) or dragsters are good for exercise, but do not let your hamster get too tired. Never leave your hamster on his own when he is playing in a toy of this type.

56 Give your hamster a chance to explore his new home when you arrive back from the pet store. Give him a couple of days to settle before you try to handle him.

57 The first step to taming your hamster is to stroke him in his home, so that he gets used to your smell. You can follow this up by offering a food treat. This will help him to trust you.

58 When your hamster accepts your hand offering food, you can pick him up. Use both hands to lift him, and hold him from underneath with cupped hands (pictured below). In time, your hamster will run from hand to hand.

59 Make sure you are sitting when you take your hamster out for handling sessions, so if he does jump, he will land in your lap.

60 Be very careful if you allow your hamster to run loose during play sessions. Tiny and quick-moving, he can escape into the smallest of gaps, and can cause a lot of damage by chewing furniture and gnawing through electric wires, as well as being at risk himself.

61 If you have any other pets, such as a cat or a dog, make sure they are in another room when you take your hamster out of his home.

62 Pet hamsters are usually fed on a mixture of seed, grain and nuts (pictured below) which you can buy at the pet store.

63 A pellet food, which provides a complete diet, is also suitable.

64 Do not buy huge quantities of food at a time. The vitamin levels in a hamster mix start to go down if it is stored for too long.

65 Store the mix in a dry place. Damp food may go off and cause stomach upsets. This is especially true of peanuts which can develop a highly poisonous mould called aflatoxin.

66 Your hamster does not need extra food, but you can provide a bit of variety in his diet. Green food, such as clover, dandelion, groundsel and salad food, is enjoyed.

67 Do not feed too much green food, as it can cause an upset stomach.

68 Brazil nuts (pictured below) are a great favourite, and are good for your hamster's teeth.

69 Hard-boiled egg, biscuit and cake are okay to feed as occasional treats. Never feed chocolate or toffee as these could clog up the cheek pouches.

70 Hamsters have their own 'language', and if you can understand it, you will know how your hamster is feeling.

71 Teeth chattering is a sign of annoyance. If you see your hamster doing this, leave him alone or you may get bitten.

72 A hamster that is standing and staring (pictured left) has heard something interesting. Hamsters have very good hearing.

73 Dwarf hamsters communicate with each other by high-pitched squeaks which we cannot hear.

74 If a Syrian hamster screams at a high pitch, it means he is very frightened.

75 Your hamster will work at keeping his home clean by choosing a 'toilet area'. This will need to be cleaned every day.

76 Some hamsters will use a jam-jar, positioned on its side, as a toilet. This will also need to be cleaned daily.

77 Once a week, you will need to do a thorough clean-out, removing dirty bedding and hidden food that may be going rotten.

78 A hamster looks after himself by grooming his own coat (pictured below). He does this by licking his paws, and then scratching or rubbing his coat.

79 A long-haired Syrian may need to have the bedding brushed from his coat. This should be done with a soft toothbrush (pictured above).

80 Dwarf hamsters, particularly Dwarf Russians, will use a dish filled with sand to roll in. This gets rid of greasiness in the coat.

81 Hamster teeth grow all the time, but they wear down naturally if you provide plenty of things to gnaw on. Gnawing blocks are available at most pet stores.

82 Sometimes the teeth become overgrown, and your hamster will show signs of discomfort around his mouth. Your vet can solve this problem by cutting the teeth.

83 Nails should wear down naturally, but if they look as though they are growing too long, ask your vet to clip them.

84 Hamsters do not live very long, but they are usually healthy little animals. If a friendly hamster tries to bite you, stops eating or loses weight, he is probably ill. Take him to the vet.

85 Your hamster can be transported to the vet in a travelling box (pictured right), or you can use a small cardboard box with air holes cut into it. Make sure you provide plenty of bedding.

86 If you have a cold, try not to go near your hamster until you are better, as he could catch it. Just like you, a hamster with a cold has a runny nose and will sneeze. Your vet will be able to treat him.

87 Tiny ear mites sometimes find a home inside the ear or on the skin around the head. You can spot the problem if your hamster keeps itching in that area. Your vet can give an injection which will kill the mites.

88 Hamsters can suffer from a condition called **conjunctivitis** which causes sore eyes. Your vet will be able to treat this with an ointment that will get rid of the infection.

89 If you see wetness and staining around the tail, your hamster could have 'wet tail'. This is the result of an internal infection, and you will need to get veterinary help quickly as this condition can kill.

90 Because Syrian hamsters fight each other, breeding should only be attempted by the experienced hamster keeper.

91 Male Syrian hamsters take no part in looking after their young. For safety's sake, the father must be kept well away from the mother and her babies.

92 Dwarf hamsters are much more modern-minded. The males help by bringing food to the young, and will keep the babies warm when the female is away from the nest.

93 If a female is expecting babies, she should be given lots of extra nesting material so she can build a nest.

96 The average number in the litter is around six youngsters, although more is not unusual.

97 The biggest recorded litter of pet hamsters was an amazing 26, born in Louisiana, USA, in 1974.

94 The female gives birth just 16 days after mating – the shortest pregnancy of any mammal.

95 The young (pictured above) are born naked, blind and helpless – all they can do is feed.

100 Finely-chopped food can be given to the youngsters when they are two weeks old. They will be ready to leave their mother at three weeks.

98 The nest should not be disturbed for the first couple of weeks, or the female may turn on her babies and kill them.

101 Hamster-keeping is a fun hobby, and you can learn a great deal from watching these small creatures and looking after them.

99 The youngsters grow very quickly. They have fur by the time they are a week old (pictured left), and their eyes open at two weeks.

GLOSSARY

Alien hamster: a hamster that has no hair.

Banded: a hamster with a white belly and a white band across the back.

Burrow: an underground hamster home, that has lots of different rooms.

Conjunctivitis: an eye infection.

Dominant spot: a white hamster with spots of colour all over, except on the stomach.

Hibernation: a period where an animal sleeps or becomes less active during the winter months.

Hoard: collect and hide away.

Marked: a hamster coat that has a pattern, or contains more than one colour.

Mottled: white with patches or fine spots of colour.

Nocturnal: awake at night-time, and asleep during the day.

Piebald: a white hamster with coloured spots and patches all over.

Platinum: silver colour.

Rex: a hamster whose coat hair is slightly lifted or curled.

Roan: a white hamster with coloured hairs throughout.

Rodent: a group of animals that gnaw, including the rat and the mouse.

Satin: a hamster with a smooth, glossy coat.

Selfs: hamsters that are just one colour all over.

MORE BOOKS TO READ

All About Your Hamster
Bradley Viner
(Ringpress Books)

ASPCA Pet Care Guides for Kids: Hamster
Mark Evans
(Dorling Kindersley Publishing Inc.)

Pet Owner's Guide to the Hamster
Lorraine Hill
(Ringpress Books)

RSPCA: Care for Your Hamster
Tina Hearne
(Collins)

WEBSITES

Surfnet kids
www.surfnetkids.com/hamsters.htm

Complete hamster site
http://hamsters.petwebsite.com

Hamster council (UK)
www.hamsters-uk.org

Hamster hideout
www.hamsterhideout.com

To find additional websites, use a reliable search engine to find one or more of the following key words: **hamsters**, **pet rodents**, **hamster care**.

INDEX